D1735489

LIMITED EDITION

6̶1̶7̶ OF 449

THE ÐEVIL & THE UÑIVERSE

: ENDGAME 69 :

THE COMPANION BOOK BY
EDIE CALIE

Ach je Verlag 2019
Berlin ~ AT&Tlantis ~ Tschuri
https://ach.je

limitierte Auflage 2019

© Edie Calie – ediecalie.at
© The Devil & The Universe & Ach je Verlag
Ein Imprint der Ach je'schen Verlagsanstalt oHG

All photos by Maria Wagner – mariawagner.at
Picture manipulation by Flip Trap

Satz und Umschlaggestaltung im Verlag
Gesetzt in der IBM Plex Serif
Druck und Bindung: PRINT GROUP Sp. z o.o., Szc-
zecin

: ENDGAME 69 :

DEUTSCH

Das Licht der Dream Machine flackerte durch die geschlossenen Lider und massierte mein Gehirn. Angenehm wabernde Gefühle strömten von oben meinen Körper hinab. Oder war das bereits die Wirkung des LSD? Ich riss meine Augen auf und überprüfte die drei Ziegen, die mit mir im Kreis um die Dream Machine saßen, auf einsetzende Veränderungen. Ein zufriedenes Lächeln lag auf ihren Schnauzen und als würde sie mich beruhigen wollen, nickte Ziege D., die links neben mir saß. Ich richtete meinen Blick wieder auf den rotierenden Zylinder in der Mitte und schloss erneut meine Augen. Ich vertraute meinen Freunden, die im Gegensatz zu mir über Erfahrung mit Sunshine Acid verfügten. Das Stroboskoplicht schoss Formen in die Dunkelheit, die sich zu immer neuen Gebilden zusammensetzten ehe sie wieder zerfielen. Also alles wie immer.

Das Klicken und Klappern waren die ersten unmissverständlichen Zeichen, dass der Trip begann. Glas schlug gegeneinander, Metall kratzte über Fliesen, ein Murmeln stieg vom Boden auf und wurde von den Wänden zurückgeworfen, bis es alles ausfüllte. Wir waren nicht mehr zu viert. Ich spürte, dass sich unbekannte Wesen in unterschiedlicher Entfernung befanden. Sie wiederholten Laute, warfen sie einander zu, als würden sie auf diese Art miteinander kommunizieren. Ein Schlag auf den Rücken unterbrach meine Konzentration. Ich öffnete die Augen und sah einen fremden Raum.

„He, nicht einschlafen!"

Ziege S. gab diese Wörter von sich, die seltsamerweise sogar Sinn ergaben. Allerdings saß rechts von mir nicht mehr Ziege S., genau genommen saß da gar keine Ziege mehr. Die Köpfe von S., A. und D. waren zu nackten Eiern geschrumpft, die nur auf der Ober- und Hinterseite behaart waren – bei D. nicht mal dort. Ihr Aussehen hatte nichts mehr mit Ziegen gemein, erinnerte mich eher an deformierte

Affen. Ihre Augen lagen eng beieinander und tief im Schädel. Statt länglichen Ohren hörten sie mit knollenartigen Gewächsen an den Seiten und ihre Münder waren von zwei Wülsten begrenzt, die sie auf und zu bewegten, um grauenvolle Geräusche zu erzeugen.

„Wo sind eure Hörner?", dachte ich. Zumindest dachte ich, dass ich dachte, aber ich erschrak als auch ich Töne von mir gab. „Was passiert mit uns?"

Die anderen drei sahen sich an, öffneten ihre Münder und stießen dabei Luft aus, was schrecklich höhnischen Lärm verursachte. Auf einem Metalltisch vor uns standen Gläser mit gelber Flüssigkeit und weißem Schaum, die sie in sich reinkippten. Ihre Hufe hatten sich in jeweils fünf lange Würmer aufgespaltet, mit denen sie die Gläser umfassten. „Finger!", fiel mir das passende Wort ein. In meinem Kopf tauchten Begriffe für Dinge auf, die ich gerade zum ersten Mal sah. Aus den drei Ziegen waren Menschen geworden, die immer wieder laut lachten.

So interessant es war zu beobachten, was hier vor sich ging, so unheimlich war es auch. Und was war das für neues Vokabular, über das ich plötzlich verfügte? Mein Verstand suchte nach etwas Bekanntem, etwas, woran er sich festhalten konnte. Über unserem Tisch kreiste eine Discokugel mit silbernen Spiegelplättchen, aber das Licht, das sie reflektierte, war lächerlich schwach im Vergleich zu dem der Dream Machine. Musik! Da irgendwo war Musik. Ich hörte Trommeln, Klavier, eine Stimme.

„"Sympathy for the Devil", coole Nummer eigentlich", sagte Mensch D., übertönte den Song und entriss mir damit den geistigen Rettungsring. „Vielleicht sollten wir ein Konzeptalbum über die 60er machen."

„Wusstet ihr, dass das Logo der Rolling Stones die Zunge von Kali sein soll?", fragte Mensch A.

„Wurde bei deren Konzert nicht jemand erstochen?", fragte Mensch S.

„Ja, 69!", sagte Mensch D. „Das wäre eh besser: Manson Morde, Black Panther Bewegung, Anfang der Satanic Panic, Ende der Hippies."

„Das Ende vom Anfang", sagte Mensch S.

„The End of the Beginning. So hieß der alternative Titel in Pink Floyd's „A Saucerful of Secret" Segment ihrer Konzept-Tour "The Man and The Journey" von 69. Würde also auch passen. Ich bin dafür", sagte Mensch A.

„Ein kleiner Schritt für eine Ziege, ein großer Schritt für-"

„Oh fuck! Was denn für Ziegen?", schrie ich mit ganzer Kraft, sprang auf und schmiss dabei den Tisch um. „Schaut euch mal an, hört euch mal zu! Ihr seid The Devil & The Universe! Keine Ziege würde jemals aus dem magischen Zirkel treten und ihre Robe für diesen Hippie Schwachsinn an den Nagel hängen!"

Ich stolperte Richtung Ausgang und hörte wie Mensch A. mir verwundert: „Du warst doch immer für mehr Flausch und Rosa!", hinterherrief.

Ich trat raus in die Nacht und knallte die Glastür hinter mir ins Schloss. Die Neonaufschrift „Waterloo Sunset - 60's Bar" blinkte blau in die leblose Welt aus Asphalt und Beton. Langsam setzte ich ein Bein vor das andere und bewegte mich die Straße entlang. Trotz Nacht war es nicht komplett dunkel. Scharfe, kantige Häuser grenzten sich hart von der restlichen grauen Umgebung ab und verwandelten meine Gedanken in kompakte Würfel. Vorhersehbar und farblos rollten sie brav nacheinander durch meinen Kopf und sorgten für eine bisher unbekannte Klarheit. Ich blieb vor einem Geschäft mit der Aufschrift „Uhren und Schmuck" stehen und betrachtete die Kreise mit den drei Zeigern, die sich alle in gleicher Geschwindigkeit vorwärtsbewegten. Die langen Zeiger tickten gleichmäßig vor sich hin. „Zeit", wurde mir bewusst. „Das ist Zeit! Und jede Sekunde ist hier gleichlang." Tick, tick, tick, der immer gleiche Abstand, eine Ordnung, die alles zusammenhielt.

Ich ging weiter, ohne zu wissen wohin. Hin und wieder eilten Menschen an mir vorbei, nahmen jedoch keinerlei Notiz von mir. Ein beleuchtetes Plakat mit der Aufschrift: „Sind Sie sicher, dass Ihre Versicherung alles schützt?", erregte meine Aufmerksamkeit. Unter der Schrift waren ein brennendes Auto und eine Frau mit schockiertem Gesichtsausdruck abgebildet. Meinte die Aufschrift mich? War ich sicher, dass meine Versicherung alles schützte? Hatte ich überhaupt eine Versicherung?

Die Realität traf mich hart wie ein Pferdetritt in die Magenkuhle. Ich beugte mich nach vorne über und erbrach eine säuerliche Flüssigkeit, bis in meinem Mund nur noch ein metallischer Geschmack übrigblieb. Mit dem Handrücken wischte ich mir den Speichel von den Lippen und sah erneut auf das Plakat. Ich hatte keine Versicherung! Ich war nicht geschützt! Ich hatte nicht mal ein Auto! Ich hatte auch keinen Job und die Miete würde bald wieder fällig sein. Auf meine Ziegen-Mitbewohner war wenig Verlass, als Menschen wahrscheinlich noch weniger. Was sollte ich tun, wenn man uns vier vor die Tür setzte? Ich musste mein Leben endlich in die Hand nehmen und auf die Reihe kriegen!

Ich richtete meine Wirbelsäule auf und machte mich erhobenen Hauptes auf den Weg nach Hause. Ich wusste jetzt was zu tun war! Jeder Mensch hatte Verpflichtungen im Leben und ich hatte mich meinen viel zu lange entzogen. Damit war jetzt Schluss. Vorwärts!

Mit jedem Schritt nahm mein Plan konkretere Form an. Zu Hause würde ich sofort eine To-Do-Liste anfertigen, einen Lebenslauf verfassen, Jobangebote durchforsten und Versicherungen für sämtliche Lebensbereiche abschließen. Ich würde meinen Körper einer ausführlichen Prüfung unterziehen, Optimierungspotenzial ausmachen und ihn entsprechend trimmen. Ich würde mein Zimmer ausmisten, ein Mindmap mit Karrierevisionen erstellen und mein Gehirn mit positiven Affirmationen hacken. Ich würde leben!

Als ich an einem überfüllten Altkleidercontainer vorbeikam, pausierte ich kurz und kramte ein Businesskleid und Sakko aus einem der Plastiksäcke. Für zukünftige Bewerbungsgespräche wollte ich angemessen gekleidet sein. Dress for success. Dann setzte ich meinen Weg fort.

Als ich am Fuße des Hügels ankam, hielt ich inne. Kein vernünftiger Mensch wohnte in einem Turm auf einem Hügel! Ja, es machte Spaß von oben die Rutsche hinab zu rutschen, aber alles in allem war unsere Wohnsituation total ineffizient! Wir müssten umziehen! Ein weiterer Punkt für meine Liste.

Entschlossen begann ich die Treppe hinauf zu steigen, aber mit jeder Stufe schwand meine Kraft. Meine Beine wurden schwer, der Untergrund weichte auf, ich sank ein und kam nur langsam vorwärts. Ich stöhnte, schwitzte und als ich schließlich oben ankam, sank ich vor dem Eingang des Turms auf den Boden. Ich weiß nicht, wie lange ich dort lag und keuchte.

Ein waberndes Gefühl kroch von meinen Füßen in den Kopf. Das Ende des Trips, das LSD hörte auf zu wirken!

Was war nur aus mir geworden? Diese deprimierende Erfahrung bezeichneten sie als Sunshine Acid? Moonshine hätte es besser getroffen. Aus meiner Brust tönte ein popcornartiges Ploppen und ich sah wie die Sorgen sich von meinem Körper stießen und ins nächste Gebüsch trippelten. Angewidert warf ich die Kleidung, die ich aufgelesen hatte, gleich hinterher. Ich legte meine Hand, die sich vor meinen Augen zurück in einen Huf verwandelte, an die warme Mauer des Turms und spürte sein lebendiges Pulsieren. Ich war zu Hause! Wie ich hörte, meine Mitbewohner ebenfalls.

Von innen drangen tranceartige Trommelschläge nach außen und tauchten die Landschaft in gleißende, fluoreszierende Farben. Die Umgebung erwachte wieder zum Leben und Muster flossen über Himmel und Erde. Neue, spannende Melodien verströmten den Geruch von Masala und Kurkuma und strichen mir sanft übers Fell. Ich presste meine Hufe vor dem Herz aneinander und grüßte die aufgehende orange Sonne.

Mit leichten Schritten tanzte ich fröhlich in den Turm hinein und blieb in der Eingangshalle stehen, um den Anblick voller Freude einzusaugen: Meine drei Freunde auf ihren

Instrumenten spielend! Zum Glück war ihre grässliche Verwandlung nur temporär gewesen, hier standen sie wieder in voller Ziegenpracht. Die Räucherstäbchennebelschwaden verdichteten sich in der Luft zu klebriger Zuckerwatte, die an ihren Hörnern hängen blieb und abstrakte Spinnenweben formte. Von der Pappmachedecke tropften bunte Noten auf den Teppich, wo die Zungen der Palmpflanze sie aufleckte. Kali! 1969! Alles machte Sinn und klang fantastisch!

Ich schüttelte meine Mähne und strich mir übers goldene Horn. Als sie mich sahen, nickte Ziege D. mir zu, als würde sie sagen: „Einhorn, da bist du ja endlich!"

Ich setzte mich mit überkreuzten Beinen und lauschte ihrer Musik. Ziegen, wie schön euch zurück zu haben. Wie konnte ich nur an euch zweifeln?

THIS AIN'T THE SUMMER OF LOVE

Dröhnende Hubschrauber-Rotoren, unverständliche Funkdurchsagen und fernöstlicher Gesang eröffnen das neue Album von **THE DEVIL & THE UNIVERSE**. Erst das Einsetzen der Trommel versichert, dass es sich in der Tat um das Wiener Trio handelt, das auf **:ENDGAME 69:** in das Jahr 1969 reist. Alles neu und gleichzeitig bleibt alles beim Alten.

Bekannte elektrische Sounds, harte Gitarren und trancefördernde Drums treffen auf indische und nahöstliche Schlag- und Saiten-Instrumente wie Tanbur, Darabuka, Tablas und Santur. Wer glaubt, **THE DEVIL & THE UNIVERSE** entdecken im Jahr 1969 ihre blumige Hippie-Seite, der irrt. Genau das Gegenteil ist der Fall.

1969 tauchte erstmals der Begriff „Satanic Panic" in amerikanischen Medien auf. Eine

Reaktion auf die radikalen, gesellschaftlichen Veränderungen und die Krisen des Jahres. Das Okkulte zog in Pop- und Gegenkultur ein, die Morde der Manson Family erschütterten Hollywood und mit der „Church Of Satan" und „The Process" arbeiteten erstmals religiöse Organisationen öffentlich mit satanischen Inhalten.

What is happening to us?

Unter dem Einfluss des Vietnamkriegs, eines entgleisenden Drogenmissbrauchs und der revolutionären Bürgerrechtsbewegung der "Black Panther" verwandelte sich die friedliche Hippie-Revolution der Jugend in einen bewaffneten (Widerstands)kampf. Der Mord während des Rolling Stones Konzerts in Altamont zerstörte endgültig den Hippie-Traum vom Frieden, der wenige Monate zuvor in Woodstock zum Greifen nahe wirkte. Das symbolische Ende der Unschuld und der Unbeschwertheit der 1960er Jahre.

Turn Off, Tune Out, Drop Dead

50 Jahre nach dem mythischen Jahr des Kollaps scheinen sich 2019 viele Aspekte der damaligen gesellschaftspolitischen und transzendenten Zusammenbrüche zu wiederholen. Und so starren die Ziegen von **THE DEVIL & THE UNIVERSE** tief in die Dream Machine und lassen Kali's Zunge über das Sunshine Acid lecken.

Wie auf den vorigen Platten führte die Jagd nach Field Recordings Ashley Dayour, David Pfister und Stefan Elsbacher quer über die Kontinente. Vom kalifornischen Death Valley bis zu Hindu-Tempeln Tempeln im, von Napalm verbrannten, vietnamesischen Dschungel. Auch eine Begegnung mit dem legendären Underground-Filmer und Magier Kenneth Anger hinterlässt seine Spuren auf der Platte.

Für den Gesang zeichnen sich Christina Lessiak („Kali's Tongue") von der Band „Crush" und Medina Rekic („1969") von der Band „White Miles" verantwortlich.

Das Ziel von **THE DEVIL & THE UNIVERSE** ist es, mit dem Gebrauch der Ikonografie des Jahres 1969 und so unterschiedlicher musikalischer Genres wie Space Disco, Psychedelic Glam, Synth Pop, New Wave und Black Metal die fiebrige Stimmung des Jahres 1969 zu evozieren. Als Paraphrase auf die gegenwärtige Unsicherheit.

: ENDGAME 69 :

ENGLISH - TRANSLATED BY MATTHIAS BAUER

The light of the Dream Machine flickered through closed eyelids and massaged my brain. Pleasantly wafting feelings streamed down my body. Or was that already the effect of the LSD? I opened my eyes and checked the three goats sitting in a circle around the Dream Machine with me for incipient changes. A contented smile lay on their snouts, and as if she wanted to calm me down, goat D., sitting to my left, nodded. I shifted my gaze back to the rotating cylinder in the centre and closed my eyes again. I trusted my friends who, unlike me, had experience with Sunshine Acid. The stroboscope light shot shapes into the darkness, which assembled themselves into ever new forms before disintegrating again. Same as always, then.

The clicking and rattling were the first unmistakable signs that the trip began. Glass struck against glass, metal scratched over tiles,

a murmur rose from the ground and was reflected back from the walls until it filled everything. There weren't four of us anymore. I felt
that unknown beings were present at different
distances. They repeated sounds, they tossed
them at each other as if communicating
amongst them this way. A slap on my back in-
terrupted my concentration. I opened my eyes
and saw a strange room.

"Hey, don't fall asleep!"

Goat S. spoke those words, which, strange-
ly enough, even made sense. But sitting to my
right there was no more goat S., actually there
was no goat at all. The heads of S., A. and D. had
shrunk to naked eggs, with hair only on their
tops and backs – or not even there with D.
Their appearance had nothing more in com-
mon with goats, rather reminding me of de-
formed monkeys. Their eyes were close together and sat deep in their skulls. Instead of
elongated ears, they heard with bulbous
growths on the sides of their heads, and their
mouths were bounded by two bulges that they

moved up and down to produce horrible noises.

"Where are your horns?" I thought. Or at least I thought that I was thinking, but startled when I, too, was making sounds. „What is happening to us?"

The other three looked at each other, opened their mouths and pressed out air, causing a terrible scornful noise. On a metal table in front of us stood glasses containing a yellow liquid and white foam, which they poured into themselves. Their hooves had split into five long worms each, with which they embraced the glasses. "Fingers!" I recalled the matching word. In my mind, terms appeared for things that I was just seeing for the first time. The three goats had become humans, who laughed loudly again and again.

As interesting as it was to watch what was going on here, it was just as eerie. And what about this new vocabulary I suddenly had? My mind was searching for something familiar, something to hold on to. Above our table spun a disco ball with little silver mirror plates, but the light it reflected was ridiculously weak compared to that of the Dream Machine. Music! There was music somewhere. I heard drums, piano, a voice.

"'Sympathy for the Devil', cool song actually", human D. said, drowning out the song and snatching away my spiritual lifeline. "Maybe our next concept album should be about the '60s."

"Did you know that the logo of the Rolling Stones is supposed to be Kali's tongue?" human A. asked.

"Wasn't someone stabbed to death at their concert?" asked human S.

"Yes, in '69!" said human D. "That'd be better anyway: Manson murders, Black Panther movement, beginning of Satanic Panic, end of Hippies."

"The end of the beginning," said human S.

"'The End of the Beginning'. That was the alternative title in Pink Floyd's 'A Saucerful of Secret' segment of their concept tour 'The Man and The Journey' from '69. So that would fit. I'm in favour," said human A.

"One small step for a goat, one big step for-"

"Oh fuck! Which fucking goats?" I shouted with all my might, jumping up and knocking over the table. "Look at yourselves, listen to yourselves! You are 'The Devil & The Universe'! No goat would ever step out of the magic circle and hang up their robe for this hippie bullshit!"

I stumbled in the direction of the exit and heard human A., astonished, shouting after me: "But you were the one who always wanted more fluff and pink!"

I stepped out into the night and slammed the glass door shut behind me. The neon inscription 'Waterloo Sunset - 60's Bar' flashed blue into the lifeless world of asphalt and concrete. Slowly I put one leg in front of the other and moved down the road. Though it was night, it was not completely dark. Sharp, angular houses stood out from the rest of the grey surroundings and transformed my thoughts into compact cubes. Predictable and colourless, they rolled through my mind one after the other and provided a hitherto unknown clarity. I stopped in front of a shop with the inscription

'Watches and jewellery' and looked at the circles with the three hands, all moving forward at the same speed. The long hands ticked evenly. "Time," I realized. "This is time! And every second is the same here." Tick, tick, tick, the same duration, an order holding everything together.

I went on without knowing where I was going. From time to time people hurried past me but took no notice of me. An illuminated poster with the inscription: 'Are you sure that your insurance covers everything?' captured my attention. A burning car and a woman with a shocked facial expression were pictured under the slogan. Was the slogan referring to me? Was I sure my insurance covered everything? Did I even have insurance?

Reality hit me hard, like a horse kick in the gut. I bent over and vomited a sour liquid until only a metallic taste remained in my mouth. With the back of my hand I wiped the saliva off my lips and looked again at the poster. I didn't have insurance! I wasn't protected! I didn't even have a car! I didn't have a job either, and the rent would be due soon. My goat roommates were already not the most reliable, as humans—probably even less. What was I supposed to do when they kicked the four of us out? I had to finally take control of my life and get my act together!

I straightened my spine and made my way home with my head held high. I knew what to do now! Everyone had responsibilities in life, and I had shirked mine for far too long. That would end now. Onwards!

With each step, my plan became more specific. At home, I would immediately make a to-do list, write a résumé, search through job offers and take out insurance for all areas of life. I would subject my body to a detailed examination, identify potential for optimization and trim it accordingly. I would clean out my room, create a mind map of career visions, and hack my brain with positive affirmations. I would live!

As I was passing an overcrowded old clothes container, I paused for a moment and pulled a business dress and jacket out of one of the plastic bags. I wanted to be properly dressed for future interviews. Dress for success. Then I continued on my way.

When I arrived at the foot of the hill, I stopped. No reasonable human lived in a tower on a hill! Yes, it was fun to go down the slide from above, but all in all our living situation was totally inefficient! We'd have to move! Another point for my list.

Determined, I began to climb the stairs, but with each step my strength faded. My legs became heavy, the ground softened, I sank into it, and only made slow progress. I moaned, sweated, and when I finally arrived at the top, I sank to the ground in front of the tower's entrance. I don't know how long I lay there, panting.

A strange sensation crept from my feet into my head. The end of the trip! The effects of the LSD were wearing off!

What had I become? They called this depressing experience 'Sunshine Acid'? 'Moonshine' would have been more appropiate. A popcorn-like sound resonated from my chest and I saw the worries push off my body and scurry into the nearest bushes. Disgusted, I threw the clothes that I had picked up right after them. I placed my hand, which turned back into a hoof before my eyes, against the warm wall of the tower and felt its lively pulse. I was home! I could hear that my roommates were, too.

From the inside, trance-like drum beats arose and bathed the landscape in glistening, fluorescent colours. The surroundings came back to life and patterns flowed over heaven and earth. New, exciting melodies radiated the scent of masala and turmeric and gently stroked my fur. I pressed my hooves together in front of my heart and greeted the rising orange sun.

With light steps I danced happily into the tower and stopped in the entrance hall to take in the joyful sights: My three friends playing their instruments! Fortunately, their dreadful transformation had only been temporary, here they stood again in full goat splendour. The fog of the incense condensed into cotton candy, sticking to their horns where it formed abstract spider webs. Colourful notes dripped from the papier mâché blanket onto the carpet, where the tongues of the palm plant licked them up. Kali! 1969! Everything made sense and sounded fantastic!

I shook my mane and stroked my golden horn. When they saw me, goat D. nodded to me as if to say, "Unicorn, there you finally are!"

I sat with my legs crossed and listened to their music. Goats, how nice to have you back. How could I doubt you?

This ain't the summer of love

The threatening sound of helicopter blades rotating, indistinguishable radio messages seeped in static, and the strains of a far-eastern melody open the new album by **THE DEVIL AND THE UNIVERSE.** Once the beat of the drums takes hold, you are reminded these sounds are being provided by the Viennese trio, who take us 50 years down memory lane with **: ENDGAME 69 :**

Familiar electronic sounds, hard guitars and trance-evoking drums meet Indian and near-eastern vocal stylings—exotic drum and string instruments with such delightful names as the Tambur, Darabuka, Tablas, and Santurs. If, however, you think **THE DEVIL AND THE UNIVERSE** have now officially unearthed their inner trippy-hippies, think again.

The term "Satanic Panic" first emerged back in the year 1969. Most probably as a reaction to the radical social changes and crisis happening at the time. The occult worked its way into mainstream pop and social culture with the Manson Family Murders and the "Church of Satan" grabbing headlines. And also with "The Process" operating as a first ever public religious organisation which addresses satanic content within scripture.

What is happening to us?

Due partially to the growing resentment of the Vietnam War, an increase in drug intakes, revolutionary human rights movements such as the "Black Panthers", the previously peaceful Hippy Revolution started to become more classically militant. When violence and murder were committed at the Altamont Rolling Stones concert, the Give Peace A Chance vibe from just a few months earlier at the infamous Hippy Convention also known as Woodstock, were definitely a thing of the past. What happened at

Altamont was a forbearing for a decidedly not so lovey dovey future.

Turn Off, Tune Out, Drop Dead.

It has been a half a century since 1969 but the turbulence of those times can definitely be reflected in contemporary political and social climates. With all their sensitivities about past and present heightened, **THE DEVIL AND THE UNIVERSE** are staring deep into the dream machine and encouraging Kali's tongue to indulge in sunshine acid.

As with past recordings, Ashley Dayour, David Pfister and Stefan Elsbacher travelled the continents to capture sounds only available beyond the confines of a classic studio. From the Californian Death Valley to the Hindu temples of Vietnamese jungles still ravaged by the violence of last century Napalm devastation. Also a chance encounter with underground filmmaker and magician Kenneth Anger leaves its trace on the new album.

Vocals are also provided by Christina Lessiak of the band „Crush" for the track „Kali's Tongue" and Medina Rekic of the band "White Miles" for the track „1969".

The goal of **THE DEVIL AND THE UNIVERSE**'s newest offering is to combine the iconography of 1969 with various musical genres such as Space Disco, Psychedelic Glam, Synth Pop, New Wave und Black Metal to create the fever-like haze unmistakably attributed to the vibe of the year 1969.